CONTENTS

Introduction 5

■ **Section 1: Questions**

QUESTION NO 1
Good mistake! (Why is that a good mistake? Where did that come from?) 10

QUESTION NO 2
If we know this, what else do we know? 12

QUESTION NO 3
Give me (draw me, tell me) ... and another, and another... 14

QUESTION NO 4
Odd one out. And why? Anyone got a different decision ... and why? 16

QUESTION NO 5
The answer is, what was the question? 18

QUESTION NO 6
Zoning in 20

QUESTION NO 7
Give me a silly answer/suggestion for...... 22

QUESTION NO 8
Always, sometimes, never true? 24

QUESTION NO 9
Give me a P.O.G. (peculiar, obvious, general) example 26

■ **Section 2: Activities**

INTRODUCTION TO ACTIVITY NO 1: Give it a silly name and children seem to learn it... 30

A. Café numbers 30

B. Spider counting 31

C. Bald headed man sums 32

D. Fact families 33

E. "V.I.P." (**V**ital **I**rrelevant, can I **P**roceed?) 34

INTRODUCTION TO ACTIVITY NO 2: Code cracking 35

A. Safe robbers 35

B. Crack the code 36

C. Times table codes 37

D. Fraction code 39

CONTENTS

■ **Section 2: Activities** cont.

INTRODUCTION TO ACTIVITY NO 3: Properties of numbers 40

A. Clocks 40

B. Guess the sets (Venn diagrams) 41

C. Factor bugs 42

D. Factor and multiple 43

E. Rachel's game 44

F. Factor chains 45

G. Last digit clock patterns 46

INTRODUCTION TO ACTIVITY NO 4: Inverse operations 47

A. Bi-products 47

B. Inside out times tables 48

C. Pyramids 49

D. Grids 50

INTRODUCTION TO ACTIVITY NO 5: Dice games 51

A. The dice game with 1 to 36 grid 51

B. Four rolls to 100 52

C. Don't make 10 53

D. Countdown 54

E. Race track 55

F. The nice nasty game 56

■ **Resources**

Glossary of key terms used 57

Resources for problem solving 58

How to use the DVD 60

INTRODUCTION

"Teachers are only as good as the questions they ask"

The aim in our Learning Network was to find ways to improve the reasoning skills of all our pupils; to increase pupil to pupil talk in maths lessons and to improve our own skills as maths teachers ... asking the right questions that help children engage and get started with a task, that probe thinking and that demand a higher order response.

One of our earliest conclusions was that it is not about finding the right activity as much as changing the way you present the activity. An activity itself won't make for more talk/reasoning.

How do you structure talk?

- Do you use talk partners?
- Do the children discuss things with each other before responding to your question?
- How long are your class spending on the carpet or listening whilst you teach?
- What are they doing?
- How much engagement do you demand?
- How much thinking time do you give them? Enough?
- Think – pair – share...

Have you used all the ways of answering?

- Fans (3, 2, 1 – show me)
- Cards (saying true/false, or yes/no)
- Whiteboards
- All whisper/shout at once
- Tell a partner
- Thumbs up thumbs down
- Hands on head if you know (less intimidating than hands up)

INTRODUCTION

Are you clear what a plenary is?

Plenary doesn't mean 'summing up' or 'getting together at the end'. It means 'fully attended by all members'. Plenaries don't just have to happen at the end of a lesson. A class can be 'gathered together' during a lesson to re-focus work, ask more questions...

Are you asking the right questions to stimulate interest and focus thinking? Our intention in this book is that we can help you to do just that!

Structure of the book

The first section of the book takes what we believe to be basic components of a maths questioning repertoire ... things you should be asking every lesson and that should become part of your core teaching skills. Each 'catchphrase' is followed by a brief explanation and then a list of examples to stimulate your thinking.

In order to illustrate what would be verbal responses, there are some written samples in speech bubbles.

The second part of the book is a list of some of our favourite activities – devised, refined, tried and tested during the year – that are core to developing a 'feel' for number, illustrated with the sorts of questions that will really improve the lesson. They are deliberately not organised into year groups; we found that almost all the activities could be simplified or extended for Year 1 to Year 11.

There are five categories of activities that develop this 'feel' for number:

- Activity no 1: Give it a silly name and children seem to learn it...
- Activity no 2: Code cracking
- Activity no 3: Properties of numbers
- Activity no 4: Inverse operations
- Activity no 5: Dice games

Finally there is a list of resources that we reviewed and found to be useful.

The accompanying interactive DVD can be found
on the inside back cover of this book.

N.B. Those activities that are illustrated on the DVD
are shown with a DVD symbol throughout the book.

Section 1: Questions

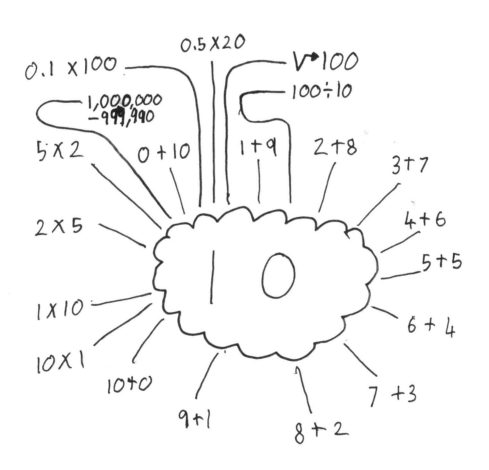

QUESTION NO 1

Good mistake! (Why is that a good mistake? Where did that come from?)

A really important culture shift is for children to accept that mistakes are how and when you learn. Make mistakes a positive teaching tool; "Can I borrow that mistake? It's really good!" As teachers we all know the common errors – so highlight them, discuss them, and then teach away from them.

Good mistakes aren't random … here are some examples you might recognise! It helps to give four answers to a question; two wrong, one right and one 'good mistake'. As you ask a question, start by asking the children to come up with the common error, the good mistake. They will soon become really good at it!

☐ x 5 = 20

100 x 5 = 20

$\frac{1}{2}$ kg = 50g

27 is a multiple of 7.

A rectangle is a regular shape.

5 2ps = 5p

A shepherd has 13 sheep and 12 goats. How old is the shepherd? 25

Writing 'one hundred and twenty three' as 10023.

Reading midpoint of 5ml and 10ml as 5.5ml.

Two minus five equals three.

3 squared = 6

0.1 and 0.99 = 1

5 x 5 = 10

70 x 30 = 210

If the area of a square 6 x 6cm is 36cm^2 then the area of a square 12 x 12 is 72cm^2.

5 x 2p = 5p

What they have done is someone has given this person 5 2p's and said it how much money is this and the child has counted the coins and not the value of the coins.

71_
43
32

They can not do it but it is a good misstake becose they foregot to take away from the band give to the Like this

6 take X 1, 11 take away 3 is 8 away 43 is 28 20

What they have done is thay wrote it how it sounds instead of whighting it 123. H T U

Writing 'one hundred and twenty three as 10023

70 X 30 = 210

This is a very good mistake. They are half right. They just forgot to add on the other zero. The trick is to do 7×3=21, then add on the number of zeros in the question!

$\boxed{100}$ **X 5 = 20**

It's a good mistake because 20 times 5 is 100, not 100 × 5 =20, they've mixed the 100 and 20 up! The right answer in the bot should be four!

oh I see what they've done, twenty seven has a seven in it so the person thought they were connected. They probably got muddled with the fives, because in the fives, the second didgit can be five (but it isn't always!)

27 is a multiple of 7

If we know this, what else do we know?

Children need to learn core facts and then rehearse them every which way. A great tool for this is the idea of 'fact families' (see page 33). Fact families tend to have three members: e.g. 3, 4 and 12 (a multiplication/division family) or 2, 3 and 5 (an addition/subtraction family). Children need to realise that learning these facts by heart unlocks masses of new facts.

4, 5 and ? are together in a family.
Could be 9 or 20.

3, 7 and 24 – which number doesn't belong? What should be there instead?
(There is more than one right answer.)

5 x 8 = 40 so
8 x 5 = 40 and
50 x 8 = 400 and
0.8 x 5 = ...
(And is 10 x 16 = 80?
Why not?)

2 + 3 = 5 so
20 + 30 = 50
What is 50 - 30 = ...

50 is 5 lots of 10
60 is 6 lots of 10...

If we know all even numbers
end in an even digit can you
name an even number over 1000?

10% of 60 = 6 so
20% = 12 and
5% = 3 and
15% = ...
and 1% = ... and
99% = ... (How would you work that out?)

1/8 of 72 = 9 so
2/8 = 18 and
3/8 = ...

If 1cm = 10mm
2 cm = 20mm
...

3 + 7 = 10 so
30 + 70 = 100 and
300 + 700 = 1000 and
23 + 7 = 30 and
57 + 3 = 60 (And does 70 - 100 = 30?)

What fact families could 4 belong to?

9+9+9+9+9+9+9 = 63   9×7=63

63÷9=7

7÷63
7+7+7+7+7+7+7+7   7×9=63   700000 × 900000 = 63,000,000,000

63÷7=9

70×90=630   9×70=630   90×70=6300

70000×
90000=
6300000000   7000×9000= 63000000   700×900 =630000

fact families   27.09.06

13 + 7 = 20   14 + 6 = 20   15 + 5 = 20
20-13=7 20   20-7=13   20-14=6 14   20-6=14   20-15=5 15   20-5=15
        13 7   20 6   15 20
7 + 13 = 20   6 + 14 = 20   5 + 15 = 20

12 + 8 = 20   19 + 1 = 20   20 + 80 = 100
20-8=12 8 12 20-12=8   20-19=1 19   20-1=19   100-20 20   100 - 20 = 80
        20   1   20   80 100
8 + 12 = 20   1 + 19 = 20   80 + 20 = 100

48÷6=8   0.6×80 = 48

6 × 8 = 48   60 × 80=4800

0.006×8000=48   0.06 ×800 =48

48 ÷ 8 = 6
60 ×8 = 480

11% of 600=66

5% of 600=30

10% of
600
= 60   20% of 600=120

12% of 600=72   1% of 600 = 6

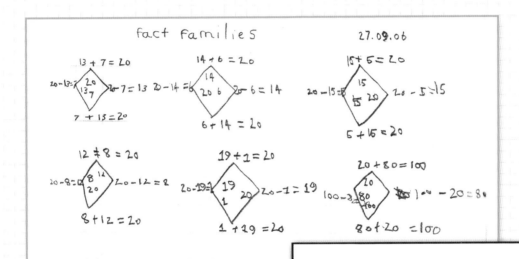

QUESTION NO 3

Give me (draw me, tell me) ... and another, and another...

The convention is to ask children for one answer. Simply asking for 'and another' 'and another' probes their thinking.

The dimensions of a polygon with a perimeter of 36cm.

Two numbers whose sum is below zero.

A factor of 60.

3 numbers with a mean of 12.

A multiple of 7.

A prime number.

Two numbers that add up to 10.

An odd number.

A quadrilateral with 2 equal sides.

A number less than 1.

A way of making 10p with coins.

A fraction bigger than $\frac{1}{2}$.

A multiple of 3 and 5.

A capital letter with a line of symmetry.

A length under 1 metre.

A net of a cube.

A rectangle with an area of 12cm^2.

Prompts for discussion:

■ Which questions have an infinite number of answers? Why?

■ Which questions have a finite number of answers? Why?

Factors of 40
① 20
② 2
③ 1
④ 40
⑤ 10
⑥ 5
⑦ 4
⑧ 8

there arnte uney morre

Multiples of 4
92   8
96   12
100   16
104   20
    24
thes will 28
nevr stop 32
nevr   36
nevr   40
nevr   44
nevr   48
nevr
52
56
60
64
68
72
76
80
84
88

An odd number

1
3
5
7
9
11
13
15
17
19
21
23
25
27
29
31
33
35
37
39
41

This is COMPLETELY Pointles, Because...
ODD Numbres go on forever!

A fraction bigger than ½

$\frac{3}{4}$
$\frac{4}{5}$
$\frac{5}{6}$ . . . . .

This IS Dumb!

$\frac{7}{8}$
$\frac{8}{9}$
$\frac{9}{10}$ Boring!

$\frac{11}{12}$

$\frac{12}{13}$

$\frac{13}{14}$ This Gonna go on forever. Because....

$\frac{100}{101}$
$\frac{101}{102}$

$\frac{1000}{1001}$
$\frac{1001}{1002}$

aslong as the Denominators 1 more thant The Numerator.
Its Bigger Than ½!

QUESTION NO 4

Odd one out. And why? Anyone got a different decision ... and why?

Present the children with sets of three or four numbers or shapes. In pairs/groups, they need to decide upon an odd one out and be prepared to explain their reasoning.

Set of numbers: 13, 16, 17, 19

Possible odd one out – and reason:
16 = only even
16 = only non prime

Set of numbers: 2p, 5p, 10p, 50p

Possible odd one out – and reason:
2p = only bronze coin
2p = only even number

Set of numbers: 64, 49, 36, 24

Possible odd one out – and reason:
24 = only non square
49 = only odd

Set of numbers: 17, 2, 7, 37, 67

Possible odd one out – and reason:
27 = not prime
67 = over 50

Set of numbers: 2, 3, 23, 33

Possible odd one out – and reason:
32 = not prime
2 = only even

Set of numbers: 1, 3, 6, 9

Possible odd one out – and reason:
9 = not a triangular number
1 = not a multiple of 3

Set of numbers: circle, square, equilateral triangle, rectangle

Possible odd one out – and reason:
circle = not a polygon
rectangle = not a regular shape

Set of numbers: 2, 4, 6, 8

Possible odd one out – and reason:
2 = only prime
6 = isn't a factor of 8
4 = only square number

Set of numbers: 3, 4, 5, 6

Possible odd one out – and reason:
5 = not a factor of 12
4 = only square

Set of numbers: 6, 15, 28, 36, 66

Possible odd one out – and reason:
6 = only one digit
36 = only one that is square and triangular number
15 = only odd number
66 = only multiple of 11

Set of numbers: 250ml, 0.25L, 750ml, 250g

Possible odd one out – and reason:
750ml – not equivalent to others
250g – only measure of weight

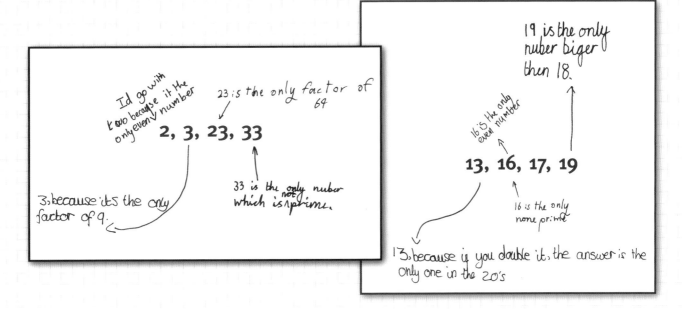

I'd go with two because it the only even number

23 is the only factor of 64

2, 3, 23, 33

3, because its the only factor of 9.

33 is the only nuber which is not prime.

19 is the only nuber biger then 18.

16 is the only even number

13, 16, 17, 19

16 is the only none prime

13, because if you double it, the answer is the only one in the 20's

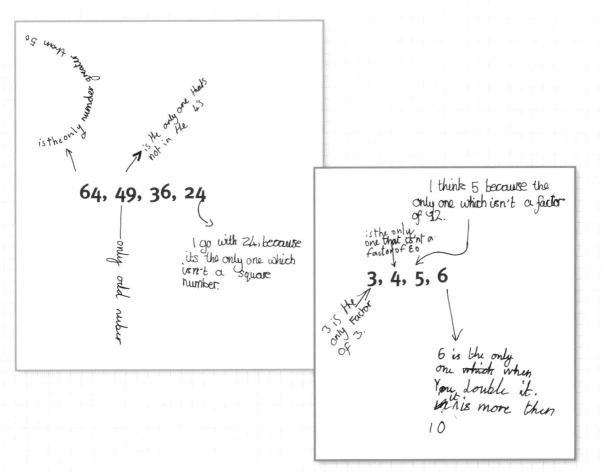

is the only number greater than 50

is the only one that's not in the 4's

64, 49, 36, 24

only odd nuber

I go with 24, because its the only one which isn't a square number.

I think 5 because the only one which isn't a factor of 12.

is the only one that isn't a factor of 60

3, 4, 5, 6

3 is the only factor of 3.

6 is the only one which when you double it. it is more then 10

 The answer is, what was the question?

This is a well-established activity. It has infinite possibilities! Circle the answer in the centre of the board and then allow paired talk and whiteboards for jottings. Set a time limit and then share responses. You can differentiate by directing some children/groups to use only division, or fractions, or to include negative numbers... Here are some possible answers to use.

24	12 remainder 5	15.3
60	Square numbers	Never
3	50%	No
15.5	The number you started with...	Always
10	The last digit is always even.	Impossible
24cm^2	48 legs	6 children

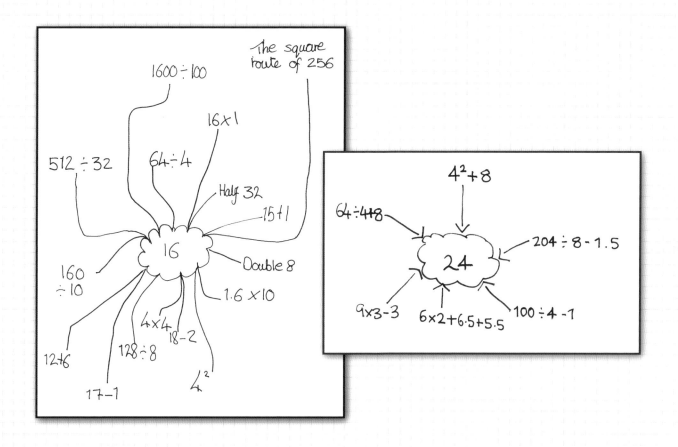

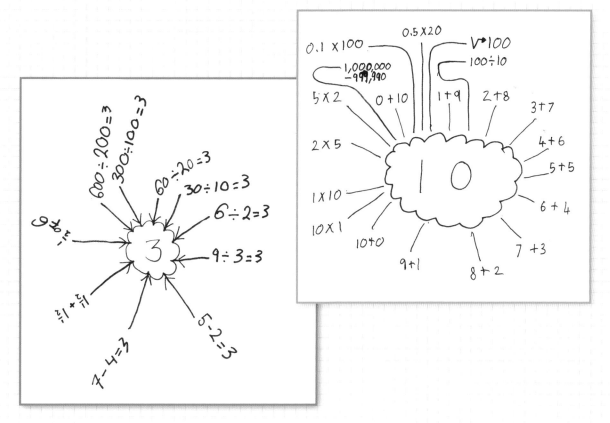

Zoning in

Explain to the children that they have to try and select a number that will fit all three conditions that you are about to reveal. Announce the first rule (condition). All children write a number that fits the first condition on their whiteboard. As you 'zone in' (i.e. reveal the second and then third rule) you can either:

- play the rule that 'you're out if your number no longer fits';

- allow changing of number to fit new conditions;

- play the rule that you circle your original number if it still fits the subsequent rule ... then two circles at the finish wins!

If you play this a few times, their first guesses become more sophisticated as they try to anticipate the additional conditions.

A number under 20 ... that is over 10 ... and even.

A multiple of 4 ... that is greater than 30 ... that is also a square number ... with both digits even. (Is there now only one possible?)

A fraction greater than 0.5 ... where the numerator is greater than one ... with an even denominator...

An odd number ... less than 50 ... that is prime ... and a factor of 50...

A quadrilateral ... that has at least one line of symmetry ... and only one pair of parallel sides ... and at least one acute angle...

A multiple of 3 ... that is also a multiple of 9 ... that is odd and a multiple of 4 ... and over 50...

Draw a triangle ... that doesn't have a right angle ... that is an isosceles triangle.

A weight under 1 kg ... that is greater then 400g ... and less than 0.55kg...

A percentage less than 80% ... that is greater than 20% ... that is more than 0.5...

A decimal fraction less than 1 ... where the digits add up to 9 ... which is greater than 0.5...

Teacher: "The first condition is a number **under 20…**"

Teacher: "…that is also **odd.**"

Teacher: "…that is also **prime.**"

Teacher: "Can anyone think of numbers **other than 7** that would have worked?"

Give me a silly answer/suggestion for ......
What can't the answer possibly be? Why not?

There are many more wrong answers than right answers and many more hands will go up when you ask for a silly suggestion! There will be the inevitable "infinity" and "forty trillion billion" but if you then ask why that was silly the child will have to reveal an understanding about the possible range/size of the right answer. Having established silly/stupid answers, ask for a reasonable suggestion and why.

The answer to 23 + 45.

I'm thinking of a number that is less than 50.

The missing number in the box ☐ x 5 = 80, 7 + ☐ = 12, ☐ x 7.2 = 97.2 etc.

How long it takes me to walk to school.

How old am I?

The length of my hair.

A fraction equivalent to 0.5

How many sweets might be in this pack?

8 + 2 + 7 + 3 + 9

The perimeter of a rectangle with sides of 4.72cm and 11.38cm.

A factor of 30.

The product of 54.5 x 77.8

A multiple of 2.

The internal angles of a triangle.

The missing number here... (see page 49)

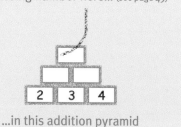

...in this addition pyramid

The lowest common multiple of 4, 6 and 16.

My silly anser could be 1 because you're adding, and 1 is less than all the numbers that I started with.

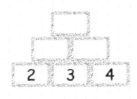

2 3 4

My silly answer would be...
5 because 5 can be made on the second level by adding 2 and 3. And the top brick has to be bigger than the second levels.

my silly answer would b 4 c1c6 because it is nowhere near the realy ansar.

My silly suggestion would by 231 because it's an odd number and 4, 6 and 16 are all even, all their multiples would be even.

"The lowest common multiple of 4, 6 and 16"

My Silly aunser would be... 31 because it's a prime number and it doesn't even have any factors

My Silly Suggestion would be 2 because it's not over 4, 6 and 16, and multiples are always bigger

my silly answer is two because it's lower than 23 and 45.

23 + 45

A a Silly suggestion wood be 10,000 because it's a very big number. much too big when you add 23+45.

a silly auswer is 22 becas it is just belo 23

QUESTION NO 8

Always, sometimes, never true?

The following are mathematical statements which may be always, sometimes or never true. Children need to learn how to prove or disprove a statement. Throw one out and allow discussion in pairs or small groups.

A pentagon has 5 equal sides.

The product of any 3 consecutive odd numbers is always divisible by 3.

Adding 18 to a 2 digit number reverses its digits e.g. 24 + 18 = 42.

Enlarging the area of a rectangle always increases its perimeter.

Multiples of 3 are always odd because 3 is odd.

The square of an odd number e.g. 7 x 7 = 49, is always one more than a multiple of 4.

Multiplication makes numbers bigger.

A prime number can't end in the digit 5.

Fractions means numbers less than 1.

All multiples of 3 end with a 3 e.g. 33 and 63.

If you divide a shape in half you get 2 pieces.

When you times any even number by 6 e.g. 18 x 6 = 108, the units digit stays the same.

If you multiply a 2 digit number by itself it makes a 3 digit number e.g. 21 x 21 = 441.

All odd numbers end in 1, 3, 5, 7 or 9.

All prime numbers must be odd.

The only 2 numbers that add to make zero are zero and zero.

Well that is only sometimes true because lots of answers are even, say 6 and 12.

"Multiples of 3 are always odd because 3 is odd"

Yeh, it goes true, false, true, false like I mean odd even odd even.

So let's say sometimes.

So it's not always true is it?

Yes of course. That's true. Like 2 x 5 = 10 and 3 x 3 = 9.

Nearly always.

"Multiplication always makes numbers bigger"

Ok, some stay the same then.

What about timesing by zero?

But what about 4 x 1 = 4?

That's true. If it did it would be in the 5x table so it can't be a prime number.

"A prime number can't end in the digit 5"

Well only 5 is a prime number then no more so let's say sometimes.

But what about 5?

QUESTION NO 9

Give me a P.O.G. (peculiar, obvious, general) example

It's all too easy to give the easiest response to a question ... challenge the children to go off the path and name an unusual example.

Name something, as below. First ask for a **peculiar** (unusual) example, then for an **obvious** one, then ask for the **general** rule about the thing.

Multiple of 3 (e.g. 111, 6, the digits always add up to 3, 6 or 9).

Numbers with a product of 60.

A quadrilateral.

A prime number.

A triangle.

A decimal fraction under 0.5

A number in this sequence 4, 7, 10, 13.

A multiple of 11.

A factor of 36.

A set of 3 numbers with a total of 10.

A set of 3 numbers with a product of 10.

Prompts for discussion:

■ Why is the answer peculiar?
■ Why is it obvious?
■ Can we be even more peculiar?
■ Can we improve our generalisation?

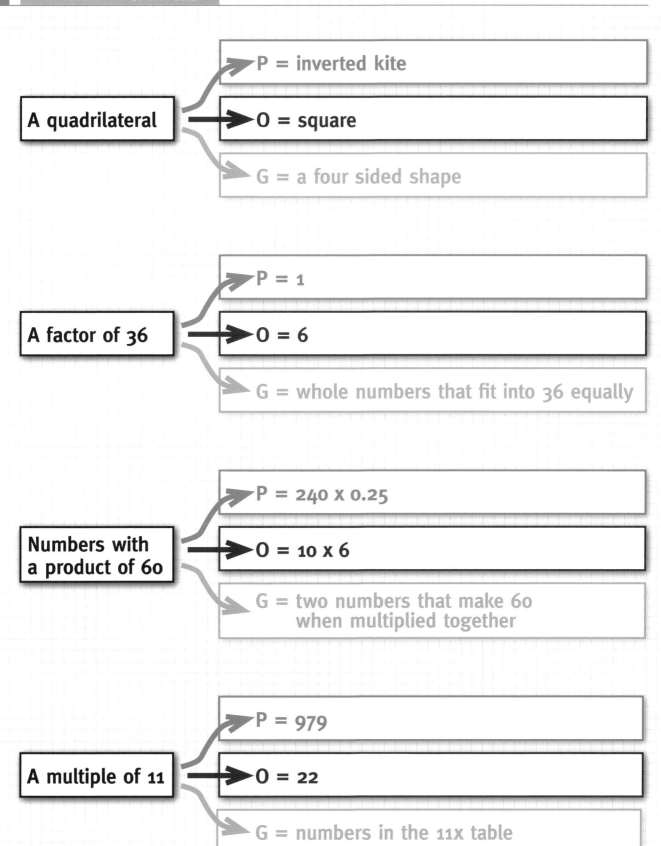

A quadrilateral
- P = inverted kite
- O = square
- G = a four sided shape

A factor of 36
- P = 1
- O = 6
- G = whole numbers that fit into 36 equally

Numbers with a product of 60
- P = 240 x 0.25
- O = 10 x 6
- G = two numbers that make 60 when multiplied together

A multiple of 11
- P = 979
- O = 22
- G = numbers in the 11x table

Section 2: Activities

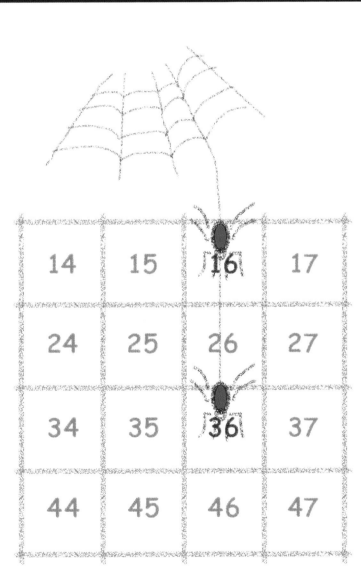

ACTIVITY NO 1

Give it a silly name and children seem to learn it...

One of the bi-products of our research and trialling was the realisation that with primary aged children at least, if something has a silly name children seem to engage with it better and remember it. Here are some examples we use.

 A. Café numbers

Instructions:

■ Multiples of 10 are like cafes, nice places to stop and rest on the journey to the answer. As the children count aloud together, mime at every multiple of 10, e.g. drinking a cup of tea, eating cake...

1 2 3 4 5 6 7 8 9

10 11 12 13 14 15 16 17

18 19 **20** 21 22 23 24 25

26 27 28 29 **30** 31 32 33

Useful questions:

■ I'm on 37. Shall I go on or back to get to the nearest café?

■ I'm on 68 ... how far to the next café?

■ I'm on 74. How many more cafes will I pass before I get to 102?

■ I'm on 31. How long since I passed a café number?

ACTIVITY NO 1: GIVE IT A SILLY NAME...

 B. Spider counting

Instructions:

- Spiders drop straight down to move, they can't count in ones on a 100 square – their movement on a 100 square would be +10. Chanting together in tens from a given number could be called "spider counting".

14	15	16	17
24	25	26	27
34	35	36	37
44	45	46	47

ACTIVITY NO 1: GIVE IT A SILLY NAME...

DVD C. Bald headed man sums
VIDEO

Instructions:

- When doing subtraction and introducing the counting up/empty number line method, if you aim for café numbers, and count in 1s and 10s, you might create "hill sums" (two jumps) or better still, "bald headed man" sums i.e. the children can doodle on their resulting calculations.

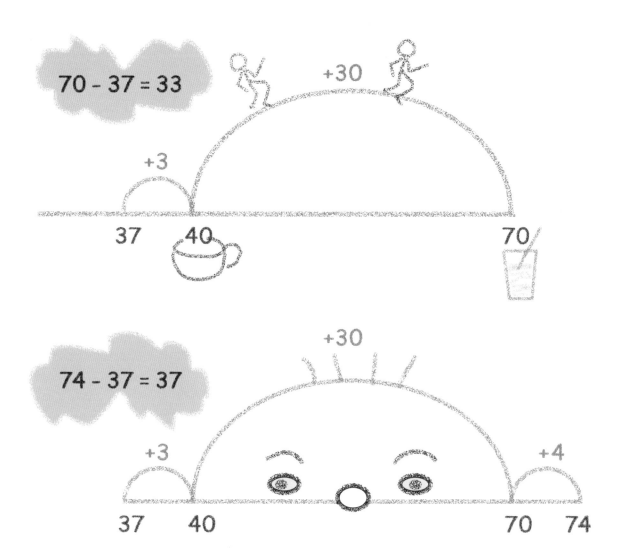

70 – 37 = 33

+30

+3

37   40   70

74 – 37 = 37

+30

+3   +4

37   40   70   74

Useful prompts:

- How far from 37 to the next café?
- Now mark the café just before 74.
- Now a big leap from 40 to 70.
- And a little jump from 70 to 74.
- Add up your three jumps ... 30 + 3 + 4

ACTIVITY NO 1: GIVE IT A SILLY NAME...

 D. Fact families

Instructions:

- Some numbers just go together, like 2, 4 and 6 (an addition and subtraction family) or 4, 5 and 20 (a multiplication and division family).

- Can the children recall all the facts in one family?

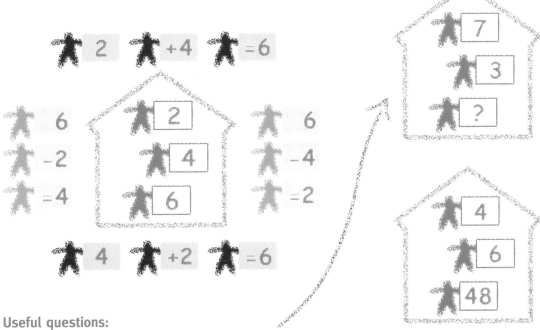

Useful questions:

- Who's missing from this addition family? Is there only one answer?

- Looks like they've got a visitor in this multiplication family – who is the odd one out? Is there only one answer to that?

Take it further:

- Sum and product families: this variation has all sorts of Key Stage 3 extensions. The top box is always the sum of the two central numbers and the bottom box always the product.

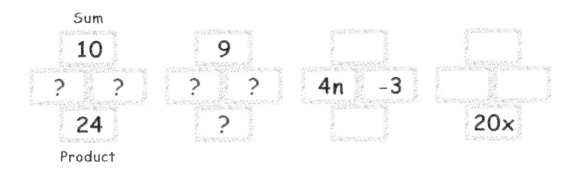

ACTIVITY NO 1: GIVE IT A SILLY NAME...

E. "V.I.P." (**V**ital **I**rrelevant, can **I** **P**roceed?)

Instructions:

▦ This is useful when doing word problems. Before starting, get the children to look at what in the written problem is **vital** information, what is **irrelevant** and whether or not they can **proceed** i.e. do they have sufficient information to answer the question.

Sarah, who is 37 next birthday, is measuring out fabric to make cushion covers for her child's classroom. Each cushion needs a length of 220cm allowing for seams. How many cushion covers can she cut from a length of fabric 4.5m long?

Shamed has collected 67 world cup stickers. How many more does he need to reach his target?

Ricky wants to buy a hamster. They cost £6. He has saved £3.50. If he gets 50p a week pocket money, for how many more weeks must he save up?

Useful questions:

▦ Can you underline the vital and delete the irrelevant?

ACTIVITY NO 2

Code cracking

The key to making this a great activity for developing talk and thinking are the questions you ask. Allow the children to develop their ideas with a talk partner then share back with the group.

You can create your own versions using one of the models here, or an excellent source is **www.activemaths.co.uk**

 A. Safe robbers

Instructions:

- Open the safe by cracking the code.
- Each letter represents a digit from 0 to 6.
- Each digit is used only once.
- The first digit is always larger than the second.

$$A + B = 8$$
$$C + D = 6$$
$$E + F = 3$$
$$G + F = 4$$
$$C + C = 10$$

A = ...
B = ...
C = ...
D = ...
E = ...
F = ...
G = ...

Useful questions:

- I think C might be a good place to start? What do you think?
- Can someone give me a silly suggestion for D?
- Letter E can't be 5. How come I'm so sure?
- So if we know that, what else do we know?
- Are you sure A is 6? It could be 2 couldn't it?

Solution: A = 6, B = 2, C = 5, D = 1, E = 3, F = 0, G = 4

ACTIVITY NO 2: CODE CRACKING

 B. Crack the code

Instructions:

- Each symbol represents a number.
- The numbers are the sum of each row and column.
- Can you work out what each symbol represents?

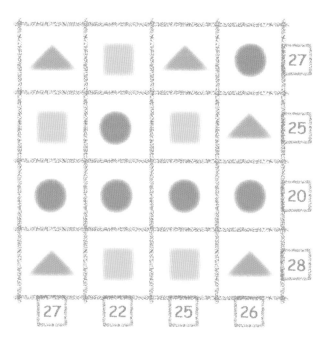

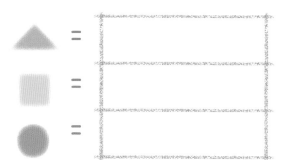

Useful questions:

- Can I have a silly answer for what ▲ could be?
- And now a sensible guess.
- Where's a good place to start? Why?
- Now where can we go?
- Could square be 8? Why not?

Solution: ▲ = 8, ■ = 6, ● = 5

ACTIVITY NO 2: CODE CRACKING

 C. Times table codes

Instructions:

■ This is the 'B' times table in a jumbled up order. The questions and answers to 1 to 9 times B are listed below in code. Can you work out what letter each digit represents?

C x B = FB   B x B = GB

F x B = GK   H x B = AB

D x B = FK   J x B = B

A x B = JB   E x B = AK

G x B = JK

Useful questions:

■ There's only one 1-digit answer. So could this be the 2x table? Why not? What else does that tell us?

■ Which question helps us? Look at J x B = B. So what must J be?

■ What about B x B? That's B squared. Its last digit is also B. What are the possible answers?

■ Is there a repeating pattern in the last digit? What does this tell us?

Instructions:

■ Here is the 'C' times table:

E x C = BE   G x C = A

K x C = GJ   C x C = K

D x C = GF   F x C = BG

B x C = C   A x C = BD

J x C = GB

Useful questions:

■ This must be a low number's table. How do I know that?

■ I think B is 1 ... and that means there are three answers in the teens. Could it be the 2x table?

C. Times table codes cont.

Instructions:

- Now have a go at the 'J' times table.

J x J = GD   A x J = FB
D x J = J   E x J = DG
B x J = EA   F x J = HK
G x J = AE   H x J = KH
K x J = BF

Useful questions:

- Where's a good place to start?
- Can we work out what D is? How?
- I think J is bigger than 5. Why might I be thinking that?
- Can we learn anything by looking at the last digits?
- Does J x J tell us anything?
- Look at J x J = GD and E x J = DG ... that's a digit reverse ... does that help?

Solution: B = 5x table, C = 3x table, J = 9x table

ACTIVITY NO 2: CODE CRACKING

DVD
VIDEO

D. Fraction code

Instructions:

- Each digit (0 to 9) is represented by one letter.
- 0 (zero) is represented by the letter O.
- Can you work out what each letter represents?
- There is a clear starting point: $\frac{1}{2}$ of E = $\frac{1}{2}$ so E must = 1.

$\frac{1}{2}$ of E = $\frac{1}{2}$ $\frac{1}{2}$ of F = E

$\frac{1}{2}$ of EF = D $\frac{1}{2}$ of D = G

$\frac{1}{2}$ of C = F $\frac{1}{2}$ of EO = A

$\frac{1}{2}$ of EC = H $\frac{1}{2}$ of IO = CA

$\frac{1}{2}$ of B = C $\frac{1}{2}$ of HO = GA

Useful questions:

- Can you see a good place to start? Why is that a good place?
- Are there any unambiguous answers? Any we can be sure of?
- EO must end in zero ... and half of it is a single digit number. Any ideas?
- HO must be 30 or more. Why do I think that? Why can't it be 20?
- D must be 8 or less. How do I know that?
- C can't be 3, or 5. Why?

Solution: A = 5, B = 8, C = 4, D = 6, E = 1, F= 2, G = 3, H= 7, I = 9, O = 0)

 ACTIVITY NO 3

Properties of numbers

Right from the Foundation Stage, children need to be talking about the **properties** of numbers ... their size, which groups they belong to, what is special about them. There are lots of games too that can be centered around knowing what is special about numbers.

DVD A. Clocks

Instructions:

▦ Working with clock faces, the children colour code numbers with coloured pencils following a given rule e.g. blue for odd numbers, red for even numbers, green for greater then 8, yellow for has a curved line in it **OR** blue for an age at our school, red for 2 times table, green for straight lines only, yellow for less than 5.

▦ You could use "multilink" and create 3D clocks building up towers on certain numbers that meet all the rules.

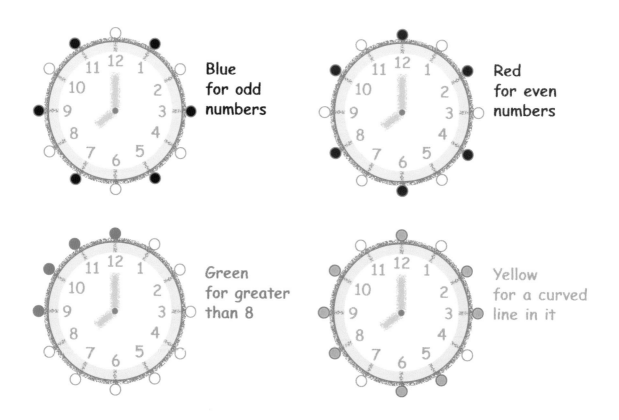

Useful questions:

▪ Will any numbers have 4 cubes on/be coloured 4 times?

▪ Can any number get red and blue? Why not?

▪ Are any numbers totally blank/empty? Why?

▪ I want 6 to get 4 cubes. Can you make up 4 rules so it does?

ACTIVITY NO 3: PROPERTIES OF NUMBERS

 B. Guess the sets (Venn diagrams)

Instructions:

- Draw a simple interlocking Venn diagram on the board. Decide upon the rule for each set e.g. even numbers and square numbers and keep it secret.

- Ask the children to call out numbers ... you place them in the right place. The class try to guess what each set is.

- Remember that some numbers will be in neither set so must go outside both sets.

- Make it competitive by seeing if they can guess both sets within 10 clues.

- Not just numbers! Stick 2D shapes on, names of children in the class...

- Get children to come to the front and put numbers where they belong as they think they have sussed it but they don't reveal the rule.

- Try: even numbers/numbers with one line of symmetry, multiples of 4/multiples of 5, odd numbers/prime, greater than 20/multiple of 3, less than 1/equivalent to $\frac{1}{2}$, square numbers/even numbers, odd numbers/even numbers, even numbers/prime numbers, triangular numbers/square numbers, quadrilateral/only one line of symmetry, has a sibling at this school/girl, wearing trousers/age 8.

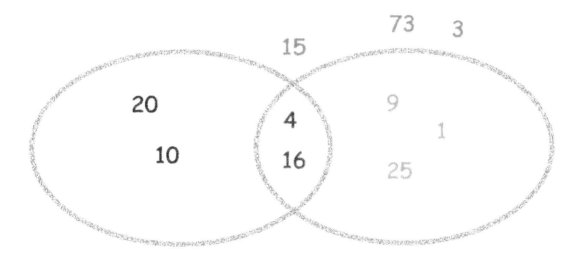

Useful questions:

- What's a good number to suggest?

- If you thought it was multiples of 4 and prime numbers, would there be any numbers in the overlap?

- I thought it might be 3x and 4x but it can't be. What number disproved that??

- What can you say about the numbers in the overlap?

- Is there an additional property to describe the numbers in the overlap?

ACTIVITY NO 3: PROPERTIES OF NUMBERS

 C. Factor bugs

Instructions:

■ This is a great way of rehearsing factors and multiples. The number goes in the body of the bug. The two 'cheeky answers' to 'what are its factors' i.e. the number itself and 1 – are always the antennae. Each pair of factors become the legs. If it is a square number its square root becomes the tail.

■ Once the children get the idea, draw bugs without the number revealed.

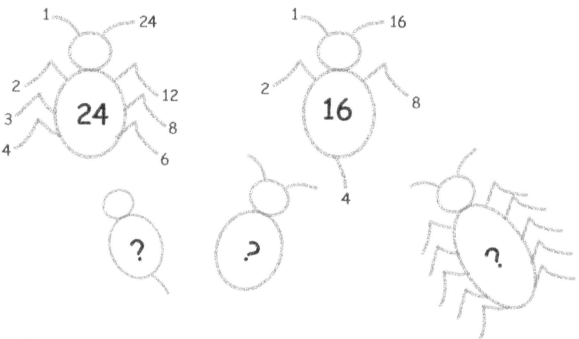

Useful questions:

■ What number might it be?

■ Can you complete the bug?

■ If it has got a tail must it be a square number?

■ Can you think of all the other numbers that would make this bug?

■ Is there a bug under 100 with five pairs of legs?

■ How many bugs with tails under 100?

■ Do all prime number bugs look the same? Why?

■ Do even number bugs always have more pairs of legs than odd? Is there an exception?

ACTIVITY NO 3: PROPERTIES OF NUMBERS

 D. Factor and multiple

Instructions:

- Work in pairs. You need a 100 square each.

- Choose a start number, any number. Note a small 1 in its square.

- Now select either a factor or multiple of that number and mark it as 2.

- Continue this process, each time selecting and marking a factor or multiple of the previous number.

1	2	3	4	5	6	7	8	(9)₅	10
11	12	13	14	(15)₃	16	17	(18)₆	19	20
21	22	23	24	25	26	27	28	29	(30)₂
31	32	33	34	35	(36)₇	37	38	39	40
41	42	43	44	(45)₄	46	47	48	49	50
51	52	53	54	55	56	57	58	59	(60)₁
61	62	63	64	65	66	67	68	69	70
71	72	73	74	75	76	77	78	79	80
81	82	83	84	85	86	87	88	89	90
91	92	93	94	95	96	97	98	99	100

Useful questions:

- How far can you get before you are blocked?

- The current best on record is 61 by Kate Emlyn-Jones and her Dad from Eleanor Palmer. Can you beat it?

- Is there a good place to start? Even or odd better? High or low number? Does it matter?

- Are there any numbers you should hold on to for as long as possible? Why?

- I've got a feeling 1 is important? Why?

- Any numbers to avoid? Why?

ACTIVITY NO 3: PROPERTIES OF NUMBERS

 E. Rachel's game *(so called because Camden's Numeracy Consultant Rachel Edwards taught it to us)*

Instructions:

- This game, for two players, uses and applies a knowledge of prime numbers, factors and multiples.

- Start with a 1 to 16 square. Player one circles a number. This is their score. Player two then crosses out all its factors and totals them, this is their score.

- Now player two circles a remaining number. Player one crosses out and scores all **its** remaining factors.

- Continue in this way until no more moves are possible. Total your score. Highest wins!

- Rule: you cannot select a number if it has no factors available.

Fatema:
1. (16)
2. 6 + 3 = 9
3. (14)
4. 5

Total = 44

Rhys:
1. 8 + 4 + 2 + 1 = 15
2. (12)
3. 7
4. (15)

Total = 49

Useful questions:

- What is a good number to start with?
- If you choose 16 what will they score? And if you choose 13?
- Will there always be some numbers left? Why?
- What is the highest score possible?
- Is it good to pick prime numbers? Why?
- Is it good to pick a high or a low number first?
- Is there a number you can pick which scores you less than your opponent? (I.e. the number is less than the sum of its factors.)

ACTIVITY NO 3: PROPERTIES OF NUMBERS

F. Factor chains

Instructions:

- Choose a start number. List all its factors and add them up **excluding** the number itself. This leads to a new number. Repeat.

16 $(1+2+4+8+16=15)$ 9 $(1+3+9=4)$

↓

15 $(1+3+5+15=8)$ 4 $(1+2+4=3)$

↓   ↓

8 $(1+2+4+8=7)$ 3 $(1+3=1)$

↓

7 $(1+7=1)$

↓

1 (1)

↓

0

Useful questions:

- What happens?
- Do all chains eventually lead to 1 then zero?
- Can you find the two numbers under 100 where something strange happens?! (6 and 28)
- Can you see why?
- Do chains start to inter-connect? When and why?
- What sort of number generates the longest chain?
- Which numbers connect directly to 1? Why?

ACTIVITY NO 3: PROPERTIES OF NUMBERS

G. Last digit clock patterns

Instructions:

■ Seeing the patterns inherent in numbers really helps children to get a feel for number. This activity focuses on the patterns created by the last digits. You need to create circle templates, as shown, marking 0 to 9 evenly spaced around the circle.

■ List a times table and underline each units digit. Join these digits in order on the circle until you get back to where you started.

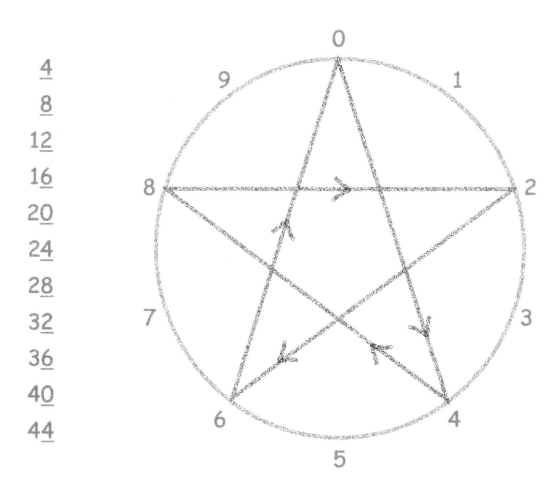

Useful questions:

■ What patterns do you get?

■ Do you think any other times table will make the same pattern?

■ I think the 10 times table might be quite boring? Why?

■ Any other times tables that will make a boring pattern? Why?

■ Do as many as you can. How many different patterns are there? Look at which times tables make the same pattern. Can you see a rule?

■ Based on this, can you make any predictions? For example, what pattern will the 14 times table make?

■ **ACTIVITY NO 4**

Inverse operations

If right from the start children learn number facts 'inside out' this really helps. There is an infinite number of activities which use and apply this knowledge. At primary level, accessible language such as 'going in through the back door' and 'un-doing' helps to explain the principle of inverse.

 A. Bi-products

Instructions:

■ Place the digits 1 to 9 in the squares. Then multiply adjacent squares and put the product on the line between them. When you have completed all the squares, add together all the numbers on the lines.

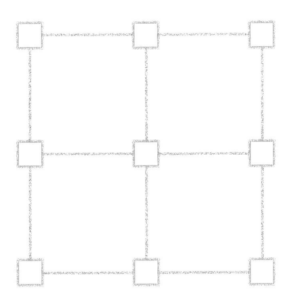

Useful questions:

■ What is the highest total number you can make? What is the lowest total number you can make?

■ Where is the best place to put 9? And 1?

One possible solution
(total = 367):

```
4 — 24 — 6 — 18 — 3
32        54        21
8 — 72 — 9 — 63 — 7
16        45        7
2 — 10 — 5 — 5 — 1
```

ACTIVITY NO 4: INVERSE OPERATIONS

 B. Inside out times tables

Instructions:

- These can be created yourself or look to **www.activemaths.co.uk** for inspiration.
- Can you complete this tables square? The numbers 2 to 12 have been used once each with <u>one number used twice</u>.

5 can't go there, can it? Why not?

This might be 3. Why?

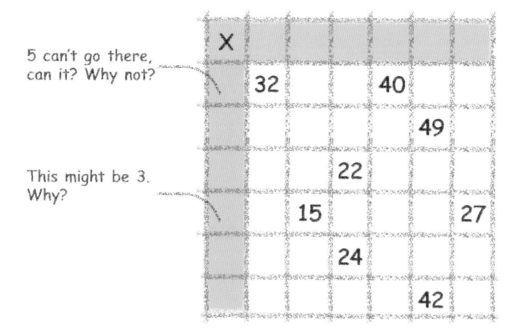

Useful questions:

- Where could we start?
- I've got a feeling 49 is a big clue. Why?
- What factors do 15 and 27 share?
- 5 goes into 15. But why do I know that isn't right for the 4th row?
- I know 3 isn't the answer for the the top row. Why not?
- Which row is least easy to start? Why?
- What are the factors of 22?
- Which numbers on the grid are multiples of 10?

Solution:

X	8	5	2	10	7	9
4						
7						
11						
3						
12						
6						

C. Pyramids

Instructions:

- This is an old favourite, made infinitely better by leaving gaps in the bricks!

- The basic pyramid is creating by putting five base bricks, and adding adjacent bricks until you create a top total.

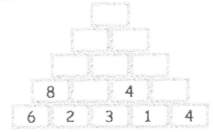

Useful questions:

- Can anyone suggest a silly number for the top brick, the grand total?

- What about a sensible guess?

- If I used only 1, 2, 3, 4, 5 – will it make a difference to the top total if I change their order on the base?

- If you think so, what combination will make the highest total on the top?

- What's the best place to put the 5?

- If a 6th brick is added, and the number 6, by how much will the top total increase?

Take it further:

- Try leaving some gaps in the base bricks (A). Can you work out what they are?

- Another variation ... use the digits 0 to 9. Create five 2-digit numbers and put them in the base. Find the **difference between** adjacent bricks as you ascend (B).

- What is the lowest and highest top brick you can create?

- Can you get zero?

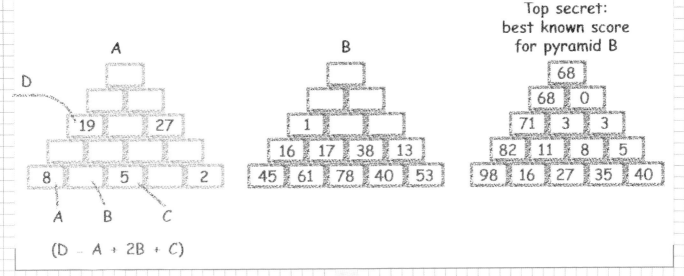

Top secret:
best known score
for pyramid B

(D – A + 2B + C)

ACTIVITY NO 4: INVERSE OPERATIONS

D. Grids

Instructions:

■ Addition and multiplication grids are familiar tasks, where the children complete the inside of a grid, adding or finding the product of external numbers. Removing the outside and some of the inside numbers makes it a far more challenging task.

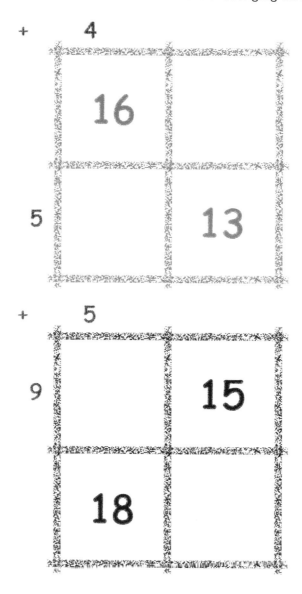

Useful questions:

■ Can someone give me a silly suggestion for what goes above the 13?

■ I think the number, above the 5, must be more than 5? Do you agree? Why?

Solution:

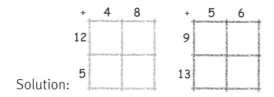

Dice games

Sets of dice are one of the most important maths resources you can have. 1 to 6, 0 to 9, small, large, plastic, foam (gather as many as you can)! Motivation doubles when playing a game, be it whole class, in a group with an adult or in pairs. These are some of our favourites. N.B. Games are much more valuable when played with an adult there who is ready to ask the key questions.

  A. The dice game with 1 to 36 grid

Instructions:

- This is a game that uses and applies times table knowledge.
- You need a set of different coloured counters each, and a dice.
- Take it in turns to roll and then cover a **multiple** of that number.
- First to get three of their colour counters in a row/column or diagonal is the winner.

1	2	3	4	5	6
7	8	9	10	11	12
13	14	15	16	17	18
19	20	21	22	23	24
25	26	27	28	29	30
31	32	33	34	35	36

Useful questions:

- What is the best number to roll?
- What is the worst number to roll?
- I have covered 20 and 27, Can I win if I roll a 4? What would I need to roll to get three in a row?
- How many numbers on the board could I cover if I roll a 6? What about 5?
- Which numbers can only be covered with a 1? Do you know what this group of numbers is called?

ACTIVITY NO 5: DICE GAMES

 B. Four rolls to 100

Instructions:

- Draw a board like this for each team.
- Teams take turns to roll a dice and record their score; they can either score what they roll, or times it by 10.
- The aim of the game, after four rolls each, is to be the team with a grand total **closest** to **100** (so over 100 can still win).
- So a roll of 6 could score 6 or 60...

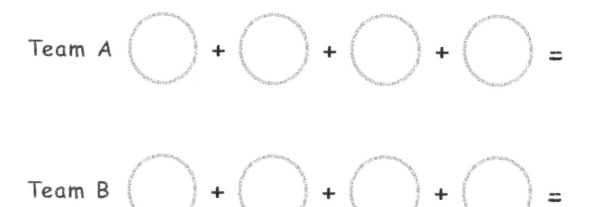

Useful questions:

- After three rolls your total is 93. They've got 79. Can you win on your last roll?
- If they then roll a 2, what might their final total be?
- Can you think of four rolls that would give you the perfect score of 100? Is there more than one way?
- If their final total is 98, and you are on 95, how many different ways can you win?

ACTIVITY NO 5: DICE GAMES

DVD C. Don't make 10

Instructions:

- You need to draw a circle and two rows of 0 to 10.

- This is a game for two teams.

- Teams take turns to select a number, from either row (it is not one row each) and place it in the circle. The number they picked must then be crossed out.

- Pick your numbers carefully because if you choose a number that makes a total of 10 with one other number already in the circle, you lose!

0 1 2 3 4 5 6 7 8 9 10

0 1 2 3 4 5 6 7 8 9 10

Useful questions:

- So if they choose 6, we mustn't choose......

- In the circle is 3, 4, 9, 9 and 8 ... am I safe to pick 6?

- If they choose 3 and then I choose 3 I'm safe, aren't I?

- What musn't you choose now?

- Can you see a way to win?

- They chose 6 – what could you choose now?

- Is there a way of winning? Can you explain it?

ACTIVITY NO 5: DICE GAMES

D. Countdown

Instructions:

- The familiar goal of this well-known TV series, is to make, or to get as close as possible to, a target number.

- A good resource is **www.subtangent.com/maths/countdown.php**. You can also play 'Who Wants to be a Mathionare' and 'Hangman' on this site!

- But you can play using old fashioned resources such as a dice. Roll five dice. All five numbers rolled **must** be used and **once only** each. Any operations can be used. Numbers may be combined to create two or three digit numbers.

- Change the rules; aim for a **type** of number e.g. a square number, a two digit prime number.

Target: 98

Useful questions:

- Now you've seen the target, anything you want me to roll?
- What would be a perfect roll?

Roll: 4   5   4   2   2

- Just looking at the numbers it feels like I'm in with a chance. Why do you think I feel that?
- I think I can make 97 – can you see how I did it?
- I can put 4 and 5 together to make 45, then x2 ... then what?

ACTIVITY NO 5: DICE GAMES

E. Race track

Instructions:

- This is a great way to encourage lots of fast mental addition.

- Each child needs a race track, two dice (preferably two different colours) and some pencils/felt pens. The race is run by rolling and adding the two dice, and colouring in the corresponding square.

- Before the 'race' begins, each child bets on which car/horse they want to win.

- Once this is done, start rolling, adding and colouring! The first number over the line wins!

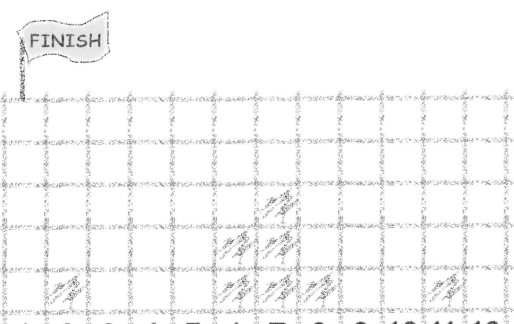

Useful questions:

- Number 1 hasn't done very well ... can you think why?

- We keep getting 7! Why do you think that might be?

- What are the ways of making 12 with two dice? And 8?

- I really want 6 to win! What could I roll to get a 6?

- Is it easier to get the bigger numbers? Which sort of size number seems easiest to get?

ACTIVITY NO 5: DICE GAMES

F. The nice nasty game

Instructions:

■ The nice version: each team needs a template like this and you, as referee, need a dice. It can be 1 to 6 or 0 to 9.

■ Teams take turns to roll the dice and then place their digit in one of their four squares. After four rolls, total each team's score. The highest wins.

■ The nasty version: this time, you roll and then place your score in **any** square in the game i.e. their squares too!

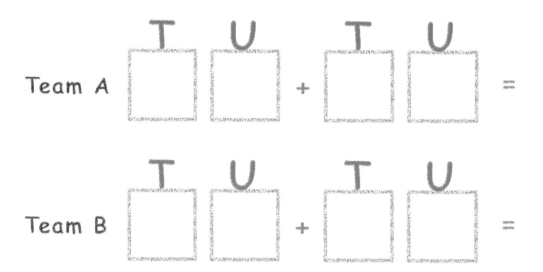

Useful questions:

■ If you're playing the nice version, where would you put a 9? And a zero?

■ If you have one final roll and 48 + ... 3 and they have a final total of 90, can you win? What would you need to roll?

■ Who is winning?

■ What does your team need to roll to win?

■ Can your team still win?

■ Instead, aim for the lowest total or the total closest to 50, or play with three digit numbers.

Glossary of key terms used

Helping children to use mathematical words with ease is a key part of building confidence. These are all words which are core to developing an ease and agility with number.

Multiple
Multiples are obtained by multiplication. Multiples of a number are what you make (MM). 12 and 16 are multiples of 4. There will be no remainder if you divide a multiple of 4, e.g. 56, by 4. It is a really important word to use so that right from the start of learning times tables so that children think beyond 10x and learn how to spot multiples and to reason what might be a multiple of a number.

Factor
Factors are sort of the opposite ... factors fit into a number exactly (FF). The factors of 30 are 1, 2, 3, 5, 10, 15 and 30. There are always two 'cheeky answers' to 'give me a factor of' ... which are 1 and the number itself.

Product
The product is the result of multiplying two numbers together e.g. 3 x 4 = 12. The product of 3 and 4 is 12.

Sum
The sum of two numbers is the result of adding two numbers together e.g. 3 + 4 = 7. The sum of 3 and 4 is 7.

Triangular numbers
A lesser used sequence but fun to know. These are generated by adding consecutive numbers i.e. 0 + 1, 0 + 1 + 2, 0 + 1 + 2 + 3, 0 + 1 + 2 + 3 + 4. The sequence is 1, 3, 6, 10, 15, 21...

Digit
There are 10 digits, 0 to 9. Numbers are made up of combinations of digits and their value depends on their place in the number. Children should be encouraged to talk about 'the last digit' rather than 'the number at the end'. This is a key way of describing multiples e.g. 'I know it's a multiple of 5 because the last digit is a 0'.

Prime
Prime numbers have only two factors – themselves and 1. Two is the only even prime number and 1 is not a prime number. Slightly pedantic, but it has only one factor. All other numbers are called composite numbers; they are composed of lots of numbers.

Square numbers
Perfect squares (square numbers) are the product of multiplying a whole number by itself e.g. 16 = 4 x 4. The sequence is 1, 4, 9, 16, 25, 36 and so on. This is an important sequence to learn.

Polygon
A straight sided closed shape with three or more sides.

Regular polygon
A shape in which all sides are equal length and all internal angles are equal. Thus a rectangle is not a regular shape! The only regular quadrilateral is the square.

RESOURCES

Resources for problem solving

Key places to source books

- www.beam.co.uk
  Beam Education

- www.atm.org.uk
  The Association of Teachers of Maths

- www.tarquin-books.demon.co.uk
  Tarquin

- www.smilemathematics.co.uk
  Smile Maths

- www.shropshire.gov.uk
  Shropshire County Council. Search for 'maths publications'.

- The National Numeracy Strategy Publication: "Mathematical Challenges for Able Pupils in Key Stages 1 and 2". Use with all abilities. Call 0845 6022260 and quote ref DfEE 0083/2000.

Other good websites

- www.tes.co.uk/teacher/brainteasers/
  All written by Anita Straker. This is a huge archive of the weekly problems in the Teacher magazine of the TES.

- www.primarygames.co.uk

- www.activemaths.co.uk
  Great source of whiteboard material and core problems. Site licence very cheap.

- www.geocities.com/Athens/ agora/2160/
  To source alphametics and cryptarithms.

- www.beam.co.uk
  Follow links to maths of the month.

- www.nrich.maths.org

RESOURCES

Resources for problem solving cont.

Books

- Author: Brian Bolt
  Title: "Mathematical Activities"
  and many more

- Author: Jon Millington
  Title: "The Number Detective"
  and "Mathematical Snacks"

- Author: Lorraine Mottershead
  Title: "Investigations in Maths"
  and many more

- Author: Anita Straker
  Title: "Mental Maths for Ages 7 to 9"
  and "Mental Maths for Ages 9 to 11"

- Author: Ken Milton
  Title: "Number Skills in Problem
  Solving" and "Children Think"

- Authors: Pat Lilburn & Pam Rawson
  Title: "Problematics"

- Author: Wilson Ransome
  Title: "Number Cell Challenges"

- Author: Roy Mullins
  Title: "Number Puzzler"

- Author: Leone Burton
  Title: "Thinking Things Through"

- Author: Jon Millington
  Title: "Mathematical Snacks"

- Author: Vivien Lucas
  Title: "A Puzzle a Day"

- Author: David Wells
  Title: "Can You Solve These?"
  (three books in the series)

- Author: Chris Maslanka
  Title: "The Little Book of Puzzles"
  (does weekly puzzle column
  in Guardian)

- Author: Professor Smudge
  Title: "Maths Medicine"

- Author: Lagoon Books
  Title: "Mind Bending Logic Puzzles"

- Publisher: MENSA
  Publications: lots of great
  puzzles compendiums

The crocodile always wants the bigger dinner

YUM

How to use the DVD

In order to illustrate and further explain some of the activities in this book, we have made a DVD. It will work in a DVD player or in a computer with a DVD drive.

All those activities that are shown on the DVD are marked with a **DVD** symbol in the contents pages at the start of this book.

Instructions

- Insert the DVD.
- You will then have three options:
  - Introduction
  - Questions
  - Activities
- Press Introduction and this will take you to Kate Frood's introduction. When it ends it will bring you back to the DVD menu. Press Questions or Activities and you will be presented with the option to see the exercises.
- Click on the exercises you would like to watch. Each chapter is about two to three minutes long.

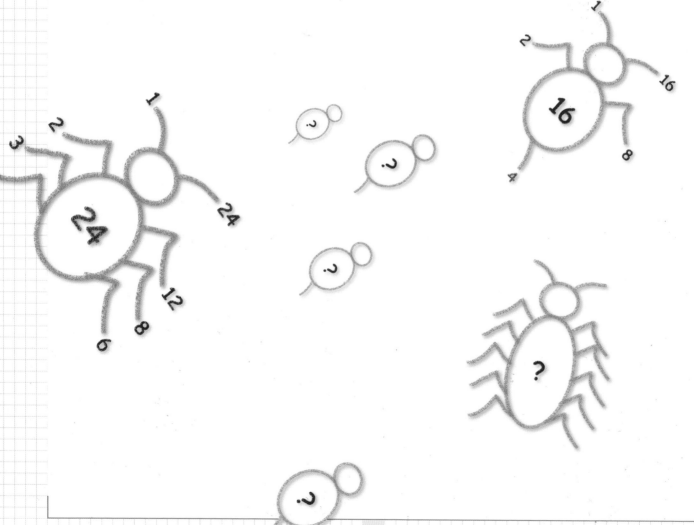